At the Construction Site

Look, a Crane!

By Julia Jaske

2 A crane can pick up objects.

A crane can pick up concrete.

4   A crane can pick up wires.

A crane can pick up logs.

6 A crane can pick up a beam.

A crane can pick up boxes.

A crane can pick up pipes.

A crane can pick up tubes.

A crane can pick up a boat.

A crane can pick up a car.

 A crane can pick up steel.

A crane can pick up wood.

Word List

crane   beam   car

objects   boxes   steel

concrete   pipes   wood

wires   tubes

logs   boat

75 Words

A crane can pick up objects.

A crane can pick up concrete.

A crane can pick up wires.

A crane can pick up logs.

A crane can pick up a beam.

A crane can pick up boxes.

A crane can pick up pipes.

A crane can pick up tubes.

A crane can pick up a boat.

A crane can pick up a car.

A crane can pick up steel.

A crane can pick up wood.

Published in the United States of America by Cherry Lake Publishing Group
Ann Arbor, Michigan
www.cherrylakepublishing.com

Photo Credits: © Engineer studio/Shutterstock, cover, 1, 14; © Sanit Fuangnakhon/Shutterstock, back cover; © Smileus/Shutterstock, 2; © Thanate Rooprasert/Shutterstock, 3; © Iam_Anupong/Shutterstock, 4; © QinJin/Shutterstock, 5; © ZoranOrcik/Shutterstock, 6; © Roman023_photography/Shutterstock, 7; © AlexKZ/Shutterstock, 8; © serpro/Shutterstock, 9; © Nordroden/Shutterstock, 10; © Gabor Tinz/Shutterstock, 11; © Iam_Anupong/Shutterstock, 12; © Mabeline72/Shutterstock, 13

Cherry Blossom Press is an imprint of Cherry Lake Publishing Group.

Library of Congress Cataloging-in-Publication Data

Names: Jaske, Julia, author.
Title: Look, a crane! / by Julia Jaske.
Description: Ann Arbor, Michigan : Cherry Lake Publishing, [2021] | Series:
    At the construction site
Identifiers: LCCN 2021007799 (print) | LCCN 2021007800 (ebook) | ISBN
    9781534188181 (paperback) | ISBN 9781534189584 (pdf) | ISBN
    9781534190986 (ebook)
Subjects: LCSH: Cranes, derricks, etc.—Juvenile literature.
Classification: LCC TJ1363 .J37 2021 (print) | LCC TJ1363 (ebook) | DDC
    621.8/73—dc23
LC record available at https://lccn.loc.gov/2021007799
LC ebook record available at https://lccn.loc.gov/2021007800

Printed in the United States of America
Corporate Graphics